Primary Phonics®

Comprehension Workbook 6

Thinking about Mac and Tab

EDUCATORS PUBLISHING SERVICE
Cambridge and Toronto

Text by Karen L. Smith

Illustrations by George Hamblin

Edited by Wendy Drexler

Cover Design by Creative Pages, Inc.

. . . .

Printed in U.S.A.
ISBN 978-0-8388-2387-3

1 2 3 4 5 PPG 11 10 09 08 07

Contents

Match.

"Let's sit in those seats in the center of that bench near the fence," said Cecil.

Her next bag fell inside the square!

Alice got a flower painted on her cheek.

Circle the best answer.

What did Mrs. Pace do at the fair?

    a. helped at the bean-toss booth

    b. ate the hot dogs

    c. painted faces

Fill in the puzzle with the correct words.

Across

1. They watched their pal Cedric in a _____. (page 3)

3. "I bet you had a _____ of pizza," Alice said. (page 15)

Down

2. Alice came back with _____ sticks. (page 12)

4. Alice gave Mr. Clancy ten _____ for the bean-toss game. (page 6)

Draw or write.

What prize did Alice pick after the bean toss?

Match.

"I want to dance in the grass."

Paige ran up the stairs to her bedroom.

Mom put a large leaf of cabbage in the garbage can.

Choose the best answer.

Where did Mom find the gyroscope?

    a. in the garbage can

    b. in the bedroom

    c. in the kitchen

Fill in the puzzle with the correct words.

Across

1. Mom put a

_____ leaf

of cabbage in the

garbage can.

(page 2)

3. She put an

_____ peel

in the garbage. (page 1)

Down

2. "Let's take the _____ can to

the street." (page 16)

4. "I will help you," said Mom, "but you

_____ to help me after that." (page 12)

Draw or write.

What did Mom and Paige do after they took out the garbage?

Hedgehog Lodge

Match.

Steve felt so small next to the tall trees.

They made some friends, too.

Then Steve gave his mom and his dad hugs.

· ·

Choose the best answer.

What did the boys do when they got to the lodge?

    a. swam in the lake

    b. went fishing

    c. went for a hike

Fill in the puzzle with the correct words.

Across

1. Steve gave his dog,

_____ , a hug.

(page 1)

3. When they went inside

the _____ ,

they saw fishing poles.

(page 9)

Down

2. They drove and _____ until

they crossed a bridge. (page 6)

4. They drove on a road at the _____

of the lake. (page 7)

Draw or write.

What did Steve and Greg do after dinner?

Match.

Sollie wished to run
with the shelties.

"I believe you are
a hero!"

His owner had to carry
him down the stairs.

Choose the best answer.

How did Sollie show he was a hero?

    a. He ate cookie pieces from the toddler's hand.

    b. He ran into the waves to get the pail.

    c. He ran up and down the pier.

Fill in the puzzle with the correct words.

Across

1. "I can not wait until I am a brave _____ like my dad." (page 6)

3. Sollie ate the _____ pieces from the toddler. (page 8)

Down

2. The toddler _____ and dropped her pail. (page 10)

4. Sollie ran up and down the _____. (page 7)

Draw or write.

Why did Sollie open his eyes wide? (page 3)

Match.

"I wish I had eight arms to clean my room!" Conroy said.

Ramon and Mollie found their animal, the seahorse.

"The animal that I like the best is the royal penguin!"

Choose the best answer.

How does an octopus hide from its enemies?

    a. It squirts a bad smell.

    b. It squirts a ball of fire.

    c. It squirts a cloud of ink.

Fill in the puzzle with the correct words.

Across

1. Moya and _____ went to study their choice, the octopus. (page 5)

3. "Look for the animal you picked to _____." (page 3)

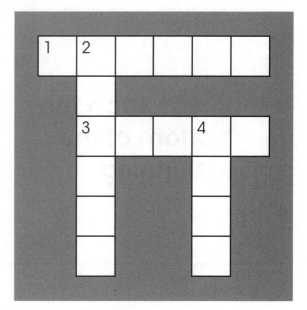

Down

2. Kai-Ying and Marge found their _____ farm. (page 11)

4. Troy and Joyce looked at the poison _____ frog. (page 4)

Draw or write.

What animal did Floyd and Roy study?

Write numbers under the boxes to show the correct order.

It was soon the bottom of the last inning.	Dwight and his uncle found seats near the outfield.

_____

_____

_____

_____

Circle yes or no.

Did Dwight hit a home run for the Mighty Mustangs?

Yes   No

Draw.

How did Dwight feel during the seventh inning?

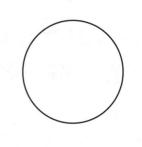

Circle the best answer.

Why did Dwight yell, "I have it!"?

    a. He had his glove for the game.
    b. The ball fell into his glove.
    c. He had his team cap at the game.

Draw or write.

What did Dwight and his uncle do after the catcher got the high pop-up ball?

Write numbers under the boxes to show the correct order.

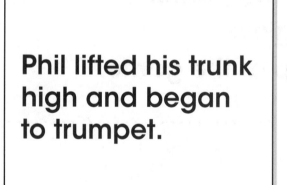

"Wait. Let me take off my earphones."

___

Phil lifted his trunk high and began to trumpet.

___

. . . .

Circle yes or no.

Was Ralph the Bird floating and swirling?

Yes   No

Draw.

How did Phil feel when Stephanie played the saxophone?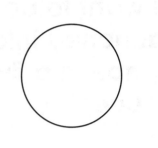

- -

Circle the best answer.

Why did Stephanie and Phil not see the crowd gather?

    a. They were lost in the music they were playing.

    b. They were lost in the crowd.

    c. Huge Humphrey was talking to them.

- -

Draw or write.

What was Sophie Snake doing when the music played?

Write numbers under the boxes to show the correct order.

"I am happy to read to you," said her mom.

"I want to be launched into space in a flying saucer."

_____

_____

"The author says that the first astronaut was a monkey."

_____

Circle yes or no.

Did her mom read Paulette a story with applesauce in it?

Yes   **No**

Draw.

How did Paulette Panda feel at the end of the story?

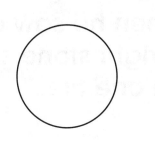

Circle the best answer.

What did Paulette want to pack for her space ride?

      a. a teacup and saucer

      b. her toothbrush

      c. a bamboo sandwich

Draw or write.

Who was the first astronaut to be launched into space?

Write numbers under the boxes to show the correct order.

_____

Then he saw a bright stone stuck in one tire.

_____

"I am going now," Andrew said to his mom and dad.

_____

"That looks like a jewel," said his mom.

_____

Circle yes or no.

Did Andrew get a reward from Mrs. Brewster?

Yes   **No**

Draw.

How did Mrs. Brewster feel when she saw her jewel?

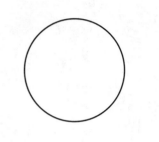

Circle the best answer.

How did Andrew find Mrs. Brewster's jewel?

a. It was stuck in his bike tire.

b. It was in the dew on the grass.

c. It was in the newspaper on his back steps.

Draw or write.

What did Andrew like to do with things he found?

Write numbers under the boxes to show the correct order.

"Turn and face the plates in the case. Look next to them in the yellow vase."

———

"Soon you will get your big surprise. Now use this scarf to cover your eyes."

———

Their mom and dad hid the clues for a treasure hunt.

———

Circle yes or no.

Did Annie and Goldie forget the candles for the cake?

Yes   **No**

Draw.

How did Goldie feel as she followed each clue?

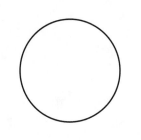

Circle the best answer.

How many clues did Goldie follow on the treasure hunt?

a. three

b. four

c. five

Draw or write.

What was Goldie's birthday surprise?